Super Smart Animals

Chimpanzees
Are Smart!

Leigh Rockwood

PowerKiDS
press.

New York

Published in 2010 by The Rosen Publishing Group, Inc.
29 East 21st Street, New York, NY 10010

First Edition

Editor: Amelie von Zumbusch
Book Design: Julio Gil
Photo Researcher: Jessica Gerweck

Photo Credits: Cover, back cover (chimpanzee), pp. 13, 14 Manoj Shah/Getty Images; back cover (dog) Courtesy of Lindsy Whitten; back cover (dolphin, horse, parrot, pig), p. 5 Shutterstock.com; p. 6 Frans Lanting/Getty Images; p. 9 © www.iStockphoto.com/Boris Diakovsky; p. © 10 M. Gunther/Peter Arnold, Inc.; p. 17 James Balog/Getty Images; p. 18 © Biosphoto/M. Gunther/Peter Arnold, Inc.; p. 21 Michael Nichols/Getty Images.

Library of Congress Cataloging-in-Publication Data

Rockwood, Leigh.
  Chimpanzees are smart! / Leigh Rockwood. — 1st ed.
      p. cm. — (Super smart animals)
  Includes index.
  ISBN 978-1-4358-9375-7 (library binding) — ISBN 978-1-4358-9840-0 (pbk.) —
  ISBN 978-1-4358-9841-7 (6-pack)
  1. Chimpanzees—Juvenile literature. 2. Chimpanzees—Psychology—Juvenile literature. I. Title.
  QL737.P96R634 2010
  599.885—dc22
                                        2009034466

Manufactured in the United States of America

CPSIA Compliance Information: Batch #WW10PK: For Further Information contact Rosen Publishing, New York, New York at 1-800-237-9932

Contents

Smart Apes

Chimpanzees are very smart apes. Apes are a group of animals that includes gorillas, orangutans, and human beings. Scientists have found that chimpanzees are more closely related to humans than they are to other apes. In fact, chimpanzees are human beings' closest animal relatives.

Scientists have also studied chimpanzees to measure how close their intelligence is to that of human beings. They learned that, unlike most other animals, chimpanzees can recognize themselves when they look in a **mirror**. Scientists also discovered that chimpanzees in the wild make and use simple tools.

People have been interested in chimpanzees for hundreds of years. These smart apes are sometimes called chimps for short. ▶

Life in Africa

Chimpanzees live in the wet rain forests and the drier **savannas** of Africa. The weather in both places is hot year-round.

Adult chimpanzees stand about 3 to 5.5 feet (1–2 m) tall. These large apes have a coat of brown or black hair. Chimpanzees can walk standing up for short periods. However, they generally walk with both their hands and feet on the ground. Chimpanzees have thumbs that work like human thumbs do. Chimpanzee thumbs are shorter than human thumbs, though. Their thumbs allow chimpanzees to pick up and hold things more easily than other animals can, but not as well as humans can.

◄ This chimpanzee is part of the Fongoli group of chimpanzees. These chimpanzees live in the woodlands and savannas of eastern Senegal.

From Baby to Adult

Chimpanzees reach adulthood and are able to **mate** at around 16 years of age. Females usually give birth to one baby at a time. The baby hangs on to its mother's belly or back for most of the first two years of its life. Young chimpanzees learn by watching other chimpanzees and **imitating** them. They also learn by trying to figure things out on their own.

As they reach adulthood, female chimpanzees often move to live with other nearby groups. However, like all chimpanzees, they maintain lifelong ties with their mothers. Chimpanzees live about 45 years in the wild. In **captivity**, they live about 58 years.

These two baby chimpanzees are playing together. Baby chimpanzees play a lot. Playing helps them form close ties with other chimpanzees.

Chimpanzee Communities

Chimpanzees live together in groups, called communities. Communities can have between 20 and 100 members. Within each community are smaller groups called parties. Adult males are the leaders of the communities. It is common for males to fight each other over group leadership. It is also common for chimpanzees in one community to fight members of nearby communities.

Within their community, chimpanzees do many things to keep the peace. The most important thing is grooming. To groom each other, chimpanzees carefully remove the dirt and bugs from each other's hair.

◀ **The chimpanzees to the right and the left are grooming the one in the middle. These apes most often groom their close friends and relatives.**

Chimpanzee Chatter

Chimpanzees **communicate** with each other using their arms and hands. An angry chimpanzee will stand on two legs, wave its arms, and throw things. Chimpanzees also communicate by making different **facial expressions**. For example, what looks like a smile to you is really the facial expression of a scared chimpanzee!

Chimpanzees also communicate by making sounds, such as hoots, grunts, screams, and barks. These sounds tell other chimpanzees if there is food or danger nearby. Each chimpanzee also makes its own special sound so that other chimpanzees know which chimpanzee is sending out the warning.

This young chimpanzee is calling to other members of its group. Chimpanzee calls can be heard as far as 2 miles (3 km) away. ▶

Eating and Swinging

Chimpanzees sleep in trees in nests they build of branches and leaves. They move through the trees by climbing and swinging by their arms. Chimpanzees climb down from trees to find food around dawn, when it is cool. The apes rest during the hottest parts of the day.

Chimpanzees sometimes hunt small animals. However, they eat mostly fruits, leaves, seeds, bugs, and bird eggs. Scientists have noticed that chimpanzees seem to use some plants as **medicine** when they feel sick. These are the same plants that people have used to get rid of headaches or bellyaches. That is pretty smart!

◀ **This chimpanzee is eating grasses. Chimpanzees often eat as many as 20 different kinds of plants each day.**

Tool Time

One reason that scientists believe chimpanzees are smart is because these apes are known to use tools. Chimpanzees use long pieces of grass to "fish" for bugs that live underground. They also use rocks to open nuts. Chimpanzees even use leaves to wipe their mouths and bottoms. Older chimpanzees teach younger community members how to make and use these tools.

In 2007, a scientist reported seeing a chimpanzee make a hunting spear by shaping the end of a stick into a point. Until this time, it was thought that only humans made weapons, or tools for hunting.

This chimpanzee is using a stick to catch bugs. It takes chimpanzees several years to learn how to do this well.

▶

Studying Chimpanzees

Scientists have learned about chimpanzees' intelligence and **behavior** by studying them in the wild. In the 1960s, an English scientist named Jane Goodall began studying a community of chimpanzees that lived in Tanzania's Gombe National Reserve. Much of what we know about chimpanzee intelligence and behavior comes from her work.

Scientists who have studied chimpanzees in captivity have also taught us a lot. For example, scientists have taught chimpanzees to use **sign language** to communicate with people. One chimpanzee, named Washoe, learned more than 200 signs. She even taught signs to another chimpanzee.

◄ **Here, Jane Goodall feeds a baby chimpanzee. She was the first scientist to discover that these apes eat meat and make tools.**

Chimpanzees are an endangered species. This means that chimpanzees are in danger of dying out. In some places, their homes are being destroyed by logging and farming. In other places, chimpanzees are being hunted for their meat.

Chimpanzees are also sometimes taken from the wild. They may end up living in zoos or being used in scientific research. In most cases, killing chimpanzees or taking them from the wild is against the law. Today, many zoos have rules that say the chimpanzees that live there cannot come from the wild. Instead, these zoos have chimpanzees that were **bred** in captivity.

This young chimpanzee is from the Republic of the Congo. Sadly, chimpanzees are now dying out all across Africa.

▶

Smart but Not a Pet!

Although chimpanzees are smart and closely related to humans, they do not make good pets! Most adult chimpanzees are too strong for people to control. These apes have minds of their own. They may decide not to follow their owners' orders.

A zoo is the best place for you to see chimpanzees. Zoos make their chimpanzee area like chimpanzees' natural habitat. There are trees for them to nest in and swing from. Most important, the chimpanzees live in a group setting. There, they can eat, groom, and play together. You can watch these smart animals, and sometimes they will watch you, too!

Glossary

behavior (bee-HAY-vyur) Ways to act.

bred (BRED) To have brought a male and a female animal together so they will have babies.

captivity (kap-TIH-vih-tee) A place where animals live, such as in a home, a zoo, or an aquarium, instead of living in the wild.

communicate (kuh-MYOO-nih-kayt) To share facts or feelings.

facial expressions (FAY-shul ik-SPREH-shunz) How feelings are shown on the face.

imitating (IH-muh-tayt-ing) Acting like someone or something else.

mate (MAYT) To come together to make babies.

medicine (MEH-duh-sin) A drug that you take to help fight illness.

mirror (MIR-ur) A flat object that shows an exact picture of something in front of it.

savannas (suh-VA-nuz) Areas of grassland with few trees or bushes.

sign language (SYN LANG-gwij) A language in which hand movements stand for words or ideas.

Index

Web Sites

Due to the changing nature of Internet links, PowerKids Press has developed an online list of Web sites related to the subject of this book. This site is updated regularly. Please use this link to access the list: www.powerkidslinks.com/ssan/chimp/

J
599.885
R

Rockwood, Leigh.

Chimpanzees are
smart!

DATE			

BAKER & TAYLOR